THE INSIDE STORY OF
SOCCER

Clive Gifford

rosen publishing's
rosen central

New York

Published in 2012 by The Rosen Publishing Group Inc.
29 East 21st Street, New York, NY 10010

Copyright © 2012 Wayland/
The Rosen Publishing Group, Inc.

Senior Editor: Jennifer Schofield
Designer: Rachel Hamdi and Holly Fulbrook
Illustrator: Ian Thompson and Holly Fulbrook
Picture Researcher: Clive Gifford
Proofreader: Patience Coster

Library of Congress Cataloging-in-Publication Data

Gifford, Clive.
The inside story of soccer / Clive Gifford.
    p. cm. -- (Sports world)
Includes index.
ISBN 978-1-4488-4847-8 (library binding)
1. Soccer--Juvenile literature. I. Title.
GV943.25.G544 2012
796.334--dc22
                        2010039702

Photographs:
The author and publisher would like to thank the following agencies for allowing these pictures to be
reproduced: cover, 16, 18 John MacDougall/AFP/Getty Images; 1, 33 Carl De Souza/AFP/Getty Images; 3,
28 John Peters/Manchester United/Getty Images; 4 Michael Urban/AFP/Getty Images; 5 Jeff Gross/Getty
Images Sport; 6 Stringer/AFP/Getty Images; 7 Antonio Scorza/AFP/ Getty Images; 8 Maxim Marmur/AFP
/Getty Images; 9 Junko Kimura/Getty Images Sport; 10 Abdelhak Senna/AFP/Getty Images; 11 Andreas
Rentz/Bongarts/Getty Images; 12 Patrick Stolllarz/AFP/Getty Images; 13 Khaled Desouki/AFP/Getty
Images; 15, 21 Adrian Dennis/ AFP/Getty Images; 17 Paul Ellis/AFP/Getty Images; 19 New Press/Getty
Images Sport; 20 Paco Serinelli/AFP/Getty Images; 22 Alex Livesey/Getty Images Sport; 23 Mike
Hewitt/Getty Images Sport; 24 Vincenzo Pinto/AFP/Getty Images; 25 Paul Gillham/Getty Images Sport;
26 Jan Pitman/Bongarts/Getty Images; 27 Clive Mason/Getty Images Sport; 29 Andy Lyons/Getty Images
Sport; 30 Sergei Supinsky/AFP/Getty Images; 31 Matthew Peters/Manchester United/Getty; 32 Toshifumi
Kitamura/AFP/Getty Images; 34 AFP/Getty Images; 35 Patrick Hertzog/AFP/Getty Images; 36 Issouf
Sanogo/AFP/Getty Images; 37 Cameron Spencer/Getty Images Sport; 38 Oliver Lang/AFP/Getty Images;
39 Phil Cole/ Getty Images Sport; 40 Stuart Franklin/Getty Images Sport; 41 Lars Baron/Bongarts/Getty
Images; 42 Ben Radford/Getty Images Sport; 43 Jonathan Ferry;Getty Images Sport; 44 left David
Cannon/Getty Images Sport; 44 right Rick Stewart/Getty Images Sport; 45 Staff/AFP/Getty Images;
46 Hachette Children's Books

Manufactured in China

CPSIA Compliance Information: Batch #S11YA: For Further Information contact Rosen Publishing, New York, New York at 1-800-237-9932

CONTENTS

INTRODUCTION

At its heart, soccer, also known as association football, is an incredibly simple team game with players controlling a soccer ball around a field and trying to score goals. Soccer has grown into the most popular team sport in the world offering excitement, action, drama, and controversy.

All Over the World

Soccer is played in most countries and is hugely popular with women and girls as well as men and boys. The game's best teams have tended to come from South America and Europe. However, large numbers of Asian, African, and North and Central American soccer players now play at the highest level and their national teams have become highly competitive. In 2001, a survey by FIFA (short for the Fédération International de Football Association) estimated that 240 million people play soccer regularly. Players enjoy the game's athletic, fast-moving action, the opportunity for individual skills to sometimes shine, and the importance of working together as a team.

TOP //// //// FACT

Soccer fans are so fanatical that they often will copy their heroes. A Japanese player at the 2002 World Cup broke his nose and had to wear a special mask for protection. Within days, around 2,000 fans had copied him!

Japan's Yuji Nakazawa and Croatia's Niko Kranjcar tussle for the ball during the 2006 World Cup.

More Than a Game

Few sports have the power to excite spectators more than soccer. Soccer fans are extremely passionate and loyal to their team, whether it is a local, amateur team, a major club, or their country playing against other nations. In the top leagues, stadiums holding 70,000 or more fans are filled week in, week out, by fans cheering their teams, while whole nations are on the edge of their seats as their team competes in soccer's biggest competition, the FIFA World Cup. Over 700 million television viewers are believed to have tuned in to watch the 2010 World Cup final between the Netherlands and Spain. The massive interest in soccer has turned top players into global superstars.

STAT ATTACK

Largest World Cup Attendance

199,850 at the Maracana stadium in Brazil in 1950.

Uniforms

One of the reasons that helps to make soccer such a popular game is that it needs very little equipment to play—just a ball and a field. Early soccer balls were made from a pig's bladder

TOP / / / / FACT

The first FIFA World Cup final in 1930 was played between Argentina and Uruguay. Both teams wanted to use their own ball and in the end played a half each with their own ball.

encased in leather, which would soak up the water and become quite heavy. Modern balls are waterproof and lighter in weight; this helps players generate enormous speed in their shots or enables them to bend and swerve the ball in the air.

A soccer player's clothing is straightforward—shorts, a lightweight shirt, socks, and shinguards fitted inside the socks to protect the front of the legs. Soft leather soccer shoes are fitted with cleats on their soles to provide the right amount of grip for the field conditions. Today, top clubs and national teams make millions of dollars selling replica uniforms, just like the one their team wears, along with all sorts of other merchandise from casual clothing to jewelry. Italian club Fiorentina even sells three types of cans filled with air taken from their stadium!

U.S. women's team star, Mia Hamm, chases the ball during a Women's World Cup 2003 match against Canada.

SOCCER THEN AND NOW

There is no one starting point in the history of soccer. The Ancient Greeks, Arctic Inuit peoples, and many others all had some sort of game involving kicking a roughly round object. Soccer grew out of various ball-kicking games in the UK in the nineteenth century and began to develop its own organized clubs and rules.

In the Beginning

The very first soccer international was between Scotland and England in 1872. It ended in a 0–0 draw, although the rematch the following year saw England win 4–2. Both matches took place without some of the features of the modern game. For example, referees and field markings appeared only in 1891 and red and yellow cards were not used until the 1960s, around the same time as substitutes were allowed.

As the game grew in popularity, there was a need for organizations to run it. FIFA was formed in 1904 and is now the organization that controls world soccer. Its first World Cup was held in Uruguay in 1930. Each continent now has its own organizing body; in the United States, for example, it is USSF. Each country has organizations that run leagues and cup competitions.

Paid to Play

At the highest level of the game, it is impossible to separate soccer from the money in the game. Top clubs now earn vast amounts of money from television rights, ticket sales, and merchandise, and spend much of their income on player transfers and huge wages. Until the 1950s, most players played for free,

Who was...

...Ferenc Puskás?

Ferenc Puskás was an extraordinary player in the 1950s and early 1960s. Short and squat, he possessed an incredibly powerful shot in his left foot, which saw him score over 80 international goals and an astonishing 511 goals in 533 games for clubs in Hungary and Spain. Puskas was a key part of the Hungarian team that went unbeaten for years in the 1950s. The team thrashed England twice (6–3 and 7–1).

Ferenc Puskás hits a trademark thumping shot with his powerful left foot.

RONALDO

Brazil fans make a colorful, noisy spectacle during the 2006 World Cup.

TOP //// //// FACT

William Foulkes was a goalkeeper for Chelsea and England in the first decade of the twentieth century. His nickname was "Fatty" but for a good reason—he weighed 310 lb. (140 kg)!

for expenses, or for very low wages. Today, a soccer superstar such as Ronaldinho earns over $25 million a year just for playing. In addition, players can earn millions more from sponsorship and advertising deals with companies. In return, they train intensely, have to deal with the media and fans, and have all aspects of their diet and lifestyles monitored by their clubs.

STAT ATTACK

Soccer Transfer Milestones

1905	$1,700 Alf Common: Sunderland to Middlesbrough
1932	$39,000 Bernabe Ferreyra: Tigre to River Plate
1961	$260,000 Luis Suarez: Barcelona to Inter Milan
1973	$1.57 million Johan Cruyff: Ajax to Barcelona
1975	$2 million Giuseppe Savoldi: Bologna to Napoli
1984	$8.5 million Diego Maradona: Barcelona to Napoli
1992	$17 million Jean Pierre Papin: Marseille to Milan
1996	$25 million Alan Shearer: Blackburn to Newcastle
1998	$39 million Denilson: Sao Paulo to Barcelona
1999	$52.7 million Christian Vieri: Lazio to Inter Milan
2001	$80 million Zinedine Zidane: Juventus to Real Madrid

AIM OF THE GAME

Soccer is an eleven-a-side game with a simple aim—scoring goals. The team with the most goals at the end of the game wins.

Game Time

A full game of soccer is played over two halves of 45 minutes, with a 15 minute long halftime period in between. A referee decides how much time to add on for stoppages such as breaking up a brawl or treating a serious injury. This added time is played at the end of each half and at senior matches, it is displayed on a board by the fourth official. In some knockout competition matches, such as the latter stages of the World Cup, teams that are drawing at fulltime play a period of extra or added time. If the scoreline is still equal at the end of this, then a penalty shootout (see page 33) is usually staged.

Bayern Munich midfielder Mark van Bommel uses the side of his foot to cushion a high ball. With a Russian Spartak defender closing in on him, he aims to set the ball down on the ground close to his feet.

Ronaldinho, playing for his club, Barcelona, hooks his foot around the ball to turn sharply. Top players have the ability to change pace and direction when they run with the ball in an attempt to beat opponents and set up a goal-scoring chance.

Goal!

In the middle of the ends of the field is the goal. It is made up of two posts 24 ft. (7.32 m) apart and is topped by a crossbar with its lower edge 8 ft. (2.44 m) off the ground. To score a goal, the ball has to pass through this rectangular box and completely cross the goal line. Judging whether the ball has crossed can sometimes cause debate. For example, one of England's goals in the 1966 World Cup final is still argued about today.

Passing and Moving

Teams with the ball in their possession look to move it around the field, aiming to get close enough to their opponent's goal and in a good enough position to score. Players can use any part of their body to control and pass the ball, including their chest, head, feet, and legs but not their arms or hands. A hand ball results in the referee awarding a free kick to the opposition or, if the player found guilty of hand ball was in his own penalty area (see page 14), a penalty. A soccer ball flies across a field so players need excellent skills to cushion and control a ball, not just with their feet, but also with their chest and thigh. When the ball is under a player's control, he can pass, shoot, or run with it.

Defending and Marking

The defending team strives to stop its opponents from scoring and also tries to rob them of possession of the ball. The team may try to tackle its opponents or pressure them into a mistake. Much of the time, defenders will mark an attacking opponent by standing close to him and between him and his own goal. Their aim is to move with the marked player, putting off the player with the ball from passing to him and denying the marked player the time and space to receive the ball and control it. Teams can mark individuals (known as man marking) or sometimes an area of space on the field (known as zonal marking).

THE OFFICIALS

A soccer match is run by the referee and his two assistants who patrol the two sidelines. The assistants help to spot fouls, offsides (see page 11), and other infringements of the laws of the game. The referee's job is a tough one but without him, competitive games could not take place.

TOP //// //// FACT

English amateur referee Brian Savill was in charge of a 2001 Great Bromley Cup game when he took matters into his own hands. When the side losing 18–1 had a corner, he could not resist volleying it for a goal and celebrating. Both teams laughed but the authorities banned him from refereeing for two months.

Female Moroccan referee Khadija Rezague—one of 50 female referees in that country.

A Referee's Role

A referee's work begins before a match when he has to assess the quality of the field, goals, and goal nets and the general playing conditions. It is the referee who decides whether to call off a match because of bad weather, crowd trouble, or anything else that could make a game unplayable. After a match, the referee has to hand in a report on the game. During a game, referees may run more than 5.5 miles (9 km) to keep up with play. They have to make dozens of decisions under pressure, from deciding on who touched the ball last when it went out of play, to whether to allow a goal or to rule one out.

The referee starts and stops the game using a whistle. He communicates his decisions to players using a range of signals. The referee's assistants indicate with flags when the ball is out of play and whether a goal kick, corner kick, or a throw-in should be awarded. They also use flag signals to indicate that a substitution is requested, a player is offside, or whether offenses have occurred out of the view of the referee.

Playing Advantage

The referee must follow the laws of the game but he does have a little flexibility in choosing how he runs a match. For instance, he may decide to talk to a player after a foul and warn him rather than book him (see page 13). He can also let play continue even if a foul was committed if, in his opinion, the team being fouled gains an advantage or benefits from the play going on. An example of this is if a player is fouled but still manages to pass to one of his strikers in a position to shoot. This is called the referee playing advantage.

Offside

One of the referee's toughest jobs is to judge the offside law. In simple terms, a player is offside if he is in front of the ball when it is played, and is involved in play with fewer than two opponents between him and the opponent's goal. A player cannot be offside in his own half if he receives the ball directly from a goal kick, corner, or throw-in. A player who is offside will see a free kick awarded to his opponents.

Judging whether a player was behind the ball or two opponents at the moment the ball was played is extremely tricky and provokes controversy in many games. Sometimes an attacker has the ball and appears to be offside, but television replays show that he was not offside but timed his run forward extremely well. Referees also have to judge whether a player is involved in active play or not.

The assistant referee, Jim Ouliaris, signals a foul by Germany's Mike Hanke on Mexico's Carlos Salcido. Playing in a 2005 Confederations Cup game, Hanke went on to receive a red card for the foul.

FOUL!

Soccer is designed to be a free-flowing game that stops only for a serious injury, when the ball goes out of play, or when a foul or infringement occurs. Unfortunately, fouls and infringements, such as tripping an opponent, time-wasting, or kicking the ball away at a free kick, happen all too frequently. The referee has to keep the game flowing and fair. He also decides what punishment to hand out to a player and his team.

Free Kicks and Penalties

Referees award one of two types of free kick when a foul occurs: direct free kicks, where the ball can be kicked and scored from directly, and indirect free kicks, where the ball must touch another player other than the free-kick taker before it goes into the goal. Any offense worthy of a direct free kick becomes a penalty if the same offense occurs inside the offending player's own penalty area.

The different fouls that see direct free kicks awarded include: kicking, charging, holding or striking an opponent, spitting at an opponent, and handling the ball deliberately. Indirect free kicks are given,

STAT ATTACK

Fouls and Cards at the 2006 World Cup

Most fouls committed: 125: Germany, France

Most fouls suffered (team): 152: Italy

Most fouls suffered (individual): 23: Luca Toni (Italy) Luis Figo (Portugal), Cristiano Ronaldo (Portugal)

Most yellow cards: 24: Portugal

Total yellow cards: 327

Yellow cards per game average: 5.11

Total red cards: 28

Dutch striker Dirk Kuyt is fouled by Portuguese defender Ricardo Carvalho during the 2006 World Cup. The match referee, Valentin Ivanov, broke World Cup records by awarding a staggering 16 yellow cards and four red cards during the game.

TOP //// FACT

English referee Graham Poll mistakenly showed Croatian defender Josip Simunic a yellow card for the second time in the 2006 World Cup match versus Australia but did not send him off. Poll went on to give Simunic a third yellow card in the match!

for example, when a goalkeeper breaks the back-pass rule (see page 15), when the player unfairly stops an opponent's movement, by, for example obstruction, or when a player plays in a dangerous manner such as by raising his foot high and close to another player's head.

Congo's Tresor Mputu (bottom) holds his head as the referee shows him a red card during an African Cup of Nations game.

Red and Yellow Cards

The referee can punish a player by cautioning him (showing a yellow card) or by sending him off (showing a red card). A yellow card, also known as a booking, is given to players for a range of offenses including time-wasting, not retreating 11 yd. (10 m) at a corner or free kick, a push or shirt-pulling, or showing dissent by being rude to the referee and disagreeing with him. More serious offenses, such as a very bad foul or a deliberate hand ball to stop the ball heading into the goal, will earn a player a red card. This sees the player sent off the field and their team must continue the game with one player less. Two yellow cards in a match equal a red card while a straight red card can also be earned by violent play. This occurred when France's Zinedine Zidane head-butted Marco Materazzi in the final of the 2006 World Cup.

Simulation

At the highest level, the referee has his hands full, with players, for instance, appealing for a corner or throw-in even though they know the ball came off them last. The most serious way of trying to cheat the referee is simulation. This is when a player pretends he has been fouled or seriously injured in the hope of winning a penalty or free kick or getting his opponent booked or sent off. Referees have to decide whether a player was genuinely fouled, or whether he has dived and is guilty of simulation, which will result in the player receiving a yellow card.

PEOPLE ON THE FIELD

A soccer field's markings and a typical lineup of a team, with one goalkeeper playing behind four defenders, four midfielders, and two strikers.

striker

striker

left midfield

center midfield

center midfield

right midfield

left back

center back

center back

right back

goalkeeper

Soccer is played on a field measuring around 109 yd. (100 m) long by 71–76.5 yd. (65–70 m) wide. Compared with some other sports, a soccer field has relatively simple markings. However, these are important since they are connected to many laws of the game.

The Field

Although artificial fields are used in training and in some leagues, soccer tends to be played outdoors on grass. Muddy, waterlogged fields tend to be a thing of the past, at least at the top level, because field preparation is now an advanced science. Many fields feature undersoil heating and artificial grass may be woven in with the real grass to add toughness. The grass used for the Sapporo Dome field in Japan at the 2002 World Cup was grown away from the stadium and moved there as an entire field.

Field Markings

The field markings consist of the boundary lines—the sidelines and goal line—that mark out the edges, two pairs of boxes, the goal area and penalty area, and a halfway line and center circle. At the middle of the center circle is the center spot from which each half of the game is started. It is also from here that the game is

Wayne Rooney waits in the technical area to come on as a substitute while the fourth official displays a board with the number of the player he is replacing.

restarted after a goal is scored. No players from the opposing side are allowed inside the center circle until the kickoff has been taken. A goalkeeper can handle the ball only inside his own penalty area. When the ball is passed back by foot deliberately by a defender, the goalie cannot handle the ball. If he does, the referee will award a free kick against him. This is known as the back-pass rule.

In and Out of Play

The ball is in play until all of it has crossed the sideline or goal line, along the ground or in the air. This is sometimes why you will see an official give a throw-in when a player bends the ball through the air down the sideline. Even if the ball's first bounce is on the field, it may have crossed the sideline completely in the air. When the ball goes over the sideline, the team that did not touch the ball last gets the throw-in. The same is the case when the ball goes out over the goal line. If the defending team touched it last, a corner is awarded to its opponents. If the team's opponents touched it last, the defending team gets a goal kick taken from inside the goal area. The one exception, of course, is if the ball crosses the line between the two goalposts and a goal is given.

Substitutes

Substitutes are relatively new in soccer. They were allowed only by casual agreement in the past and first occurred at a World Cup in 1970. Today, teams are allowed to make up to three substitutions in each competitive game. In many competitions, the team's subs bench consists of five or seven players who may or may not include a goalkeeper. Players can be withdrawn from a match for a range of reasons, from suffering a slight or serious injury to underperforming; or a defender may be replaced by an attacker as one side chases the game.

TOP //// //// FACT

At the 2002 World Cup, Cha Doo-Ri of South Korea came on as a substitute and was booked after just 20 seconds for a bad tackle. Bolivia's Marco Etcheverry holds the dubious record of being the substitute sent off fastest at a World Cup. In the 1994 game against Germany he received his marching orders after just three minutes!

THE GOALKEEPER

The goalkeeper stands alone. As the player with the best view of how an opposition attack is developing, the goalkeeper is expected to communicate instructions to his defenders and to command his penalty and goal area. A goalkeeper's saves and skills can defend a team's lead or keep it in a game. A mistake by the goalkeeper can lose the match.

Agility and Bravery

Goalkeepers train long and hard to become extremely agile and flexible. This enables them to leap high to collect the ball in a crowded penalty area or to dive wide to reach and deflect the ball around the goalpost. Goalies also need great bravery to challenge for the ball such as by diving at the feet of an attacker. The back-pass rule (see page 15) means that goalkeepers cannot handle the ball directly from a throw-in or a kicked pass made by one of their teammates. They have to use their head or feet to clear the ball.

Awareness and Positioning

Much of a goalie's game is about avoiding having to make spectacular saves. Top goalkeepers such as the Italian, Gianluigi Buffon, or the Czech Republic's Petr Cech rely on superb awareness and reading of the game to position themselves in a way that makes a save look routine or easy.

A top goalkeeper like Ricardo of Portugal may not need to act for long periods of time but, when he is needed, he must react sharply.

Behind a seemingly straightforward catch or a punch of the ball clear lie great concentration, fast footwork and good handling skills. Top goalies put in hours of training so that they learn how and where to position themselves. This includes knowing how to reduce the amount of goal space at which an opponent has to aim. They also work at placing their bodies behind the ball to act as a barrier.

Chris Kirkland punches the ball clear. Goalies pride themselves on keeping a shutout (clean sheet)—when their team does not concede a goal in a game.

Starting Attacks

A goalkeeper may be the last line of defense, but he can also be the first line of attack. When a goalie has the ball under control, he has six seconds to release it, otherwise the referee will award an indirect free kick to the opposition. In that time, the goalie has to choose where to move the ball to and in what way. This is known as distribution. The goalie can kick the ball from his hand, roll the ball out, and kick it off the ground, or use one of three types of throw—underarm, overarm, or javelin—to distribute the ball. The underarm throw is the most accurate, the javelin often the quickest, and the overarm can be used for the greatest distance. Whether kicked or thrown, quick, accurate distribution can release a teammate in space to start a useful attack.

TOP FACT

In an 1894 FA Cup game between Preston North End and Reading, it rained so heavily that the Preston goalkeeper, Jimmy Trainer, played in a raincoat!

Great Goalkeepers

Top goalies lose few of their skills even into their 30s and some of the best goalkeepers around have long careers at the highest level. In 2007, Oliver Kahn turned 37; David James, who had a great 2006/07 season with Portsmouth, was 36. Fabien Barthez retired in 2006 age 36, and the great Dino Zoff was 40 years old when he captained Italy to win the 1980 World Cup.

THE DEFENSE

A team's defense usually consists of three, four, or five outfield players. These soccer players work together as a unit to mark opponents. They also work with their other teammates to repel the opposition's attacks and stop goals being scored against them.

Jockeying

During a game, defenders will have many individual tasks to perform such as tackling, heading the ball clear, and jockeying opponents with the ball. Jockeying is where a defender aims to get close to the opponent with the ball, to delay his progress so that other defenders can get into stronger positions. The jockeying defender tries to guide his opponent away from danger areas and, once there is support, may challenge for the ball with a tackle. When an opposing striker receives the ball with his back to goal, a defender may get closer. He tries to prevent his opponent turning to face goal and hopes to pressure him into making a mistake.

Central Defenders

Strong and decisive both in the air and on the ground, a team's central defenders are the players most responsible for stopping opposition attacks breaking through the middle of the field. Since many balls are hit long and high toward their goal, nearly all central defenders are skilled at winning the ball in the air and clearing the ball upfield and away from danger. On the ground, they have to be able to react quickly to opponents' turns and runs and may be forced into

Who is...

...Fabio Cannavaro?

Fabio Cannavaro is a highly-skilled Italian defender who played for four Italian Serie A clubs before joining Real Madrid, in 2006. Famed for his superb anticipation and timing, which enable him to make clean tackles and interceptions frequently, Cannavaro has played 105 times for Italy and, as captain, lifted the 2006 World Cup. Although he is short for a central defender at 5 ft. 8 in. (1.72 m), Cannavaro is nonetheless extremely good in the air and was crowned FIFA's World Player of the Year in 2006.

Cannavaro nudges the ball out of the path of Australia's Mark Viduka.

a sliding tackle. The very best central defenders are also comfortable on the ball and can bring it out of defense, passing it to teammates, and linking defense and attack.

Andrea Ranocchia tackles Alessandro Del Piero in a 2006 Serie B match. Ranocchia timed his tackle to put the ball out of play for a throw-in.

Fullbacks

Fullbacks (also called defensemen) tend to be quicker and more mobile on the ground than central defenders, but they still need to be good in the air and able to make swift, clean tackles. They must mark and prevent opponents from playing wide. This includes stopping wingers from crossing the ball or getting past them and running with the ball into the penalty area. Fullbacks such as Germany's Philipp Lahm or England's Ashley Cole are fit, fast, and possess a lot of stamina. They need stamina since they are expected to patrol most of their side of the field and be a link in attack by making a run along the touchline (or sideline) in front of their midfield to receive the ball. Fullbacks such as England's Gary Neville, France's Lilian Thuram (retired), and the Brazilian veteran, Cafu, are particularly skilled at this.

THE MIDFIELDERS

Midfielders are often a team's most versatile players, able to both attack and defend well. They must possess large reserves of energy since they typically cover more ground in a game than any other player. A FIFA study of play in the 2002 World Cup revealed that a midfielder can run a distance of over 7.5 miles (12 km) per match.

Tracking and Tackling

Midfielders are always vital to a game. In many matches, the ball is in the middle of the field often, as both sides vie for possession. Midfielders need to be able to chase down the ball, win it in a tackle, and then use it effectively. When their side does not have the ball, midfielders have to defend by tracking opponents. This means that they stay aware of and follow an opponent making an attacking run forward, trying to mark them out of the game. When their side has the ball, midfielders are often a vital part of an attack. Some players, such as England's Frank Lampard and Steven Gerrard, are renowned for making surging runs forward to get on the end of an attack and scoring with a powerful shot.

AC Milan teammates Gennaro Gattuso and Andrea Pirlo. Both are midfielders, but Gattuso is more of a tough-tackling defensive midfielder while Pirlo uses the ball to make passes and keep attacks moving.

TOP //// //// FACT

Real Madrid had the world's most expensive midfield in 2003 and 2004, when Luis Figo, Zinedine Zidane, and David Beckham played for the team, with the three players' transfer fees costing around $187 million!

Anchors and Attackers

As the game of soccer has progressed, some central midfield positions have become highly specialized. Some teams, for example, play a midfield anchor. This is a hard-working, hard-tackling defensive midfielder who plays just in front of his defense. His job is to help protect his defense and break down the opposition's attacks. Other midfielders with superb vision and passing skills play a more attacking role, controlling play and looking for the pass that will give a teammate a great scoring chance. These are midfield playmakers, such as Italy's Andrea Pirlo or Spain's Cesc Fabregas. Some particularly attacking midfielders, such as England's Paul Scholes, rising Argentinean star Lionel Messi, or the French legend, Michel Platini, play almost as an extra attacker just behind the strikers and set up goals or score themselves.

Wide Midfielders and Wingers

Wide midfielders are expected to work hard to track their opposite number and provide lots of width in attack. Like David Beckham, they are expected to be excellent at crossing the ball from near the sideline into the penalty area. Wingers are a more highly-attacking version of the wide midfielder. They are players with the skills, pace, and tricks to beat opponents and attack the opposition penalty area either with accurate crosses or by running with the ball themselves. Typical wingers were out of fashion for decades, but in recent times, the supreme skills of players such as the Netherlands' Arjen Robben and Portugal's Cristiano Ronaldo have seen wingers back in fashion.

Chelsea's Frank Lampard drives past Fulham's Michael Brown. Midfielders can dictate the play of their side by keeping the game moving, starting attacks and finishing them off with accurate shots and headers.

TOP //// //// FACT

In 1998, with a goal against Jamaica, Croatian midfielder Robert Prosinecki became the only player to score goals in the World Cup finals for two countries. In 1990, he had scored for Yugoslavia.

STRIKERS

Strikers play a key role in their team's attacks and they are usually a side's most frequent goalscorers. In a tight match, a team's strikers may get only a handful of chances to score. They must take these and get their shot or header on target. A striker on top of his game can make the difference between a win and a draw or defeat.

Different Types

Strikers come in all shapes and sizes, from relatively small players, such as the great Argentinean Diego Maradona 5 ft. 5 in. (1.66 m) and Italian star Gianfranco Zola 5 ft. 6 in. (1.67 m), to tall target men like the Czech Republic's Jan Koller and Serbia's Nikola Zigic (both 6 ft. 7 in. (2.02 m tall). Strikers also play in quite different ways. Some strikers, such as the Ivory Coast's Didier Drogba, are strong in the air and good at keeping hold of the ball. These strikers often play as center forwards, leading the attacking line and aiming to score from headers and through their power. Other strikers, such as France's Thierry Henry and Cameroon's Samuel Eto'o, rely on their pace, trickery, and sometimes, good passes from their teammates to get behind the opposition defense or set up their teammates in attack. Some strikers, such as England's Wayne Rooney, operate all over the field and may pop up on the wing or deep into midfield to receive a ball and run at opponents.

Liverpool's striker, Craig Bellamy, 5 ft. 6 in. (1.67 m) tall, is substituted in favor of Peter Crouch in their 2006 Champions League match against Maccabi Haifa. At 6 ft. 8 in. (2.01 m), Crouch is the tallest player in the English Premier League and the tallest to have represented England.

Striking Skills

Possessing a strong, accurate shot, being good in the air, and having an eye for goal are just three of the many attributes a striker needs to be successful. Strikers must have excellent vision and awareness of the game around them. They also need lightning-fast reactions to latch onto a loose ball from a rebound or to make a darting run into space. A good striker needs strength to hold off defenders as he controls the ball, and bravery to go in for a ball in a crowded penalty area with his head or foot. Just as importantly, strikers must have confidence to put a bad miss or a lean spell, where they have gone a number of games without scoring, behind them.

Who is...
...Samuel Eto'o?

Samuel Eto'o is a Cameroon striker who plays his club soccer for Barcelona. He scored 61 goals in his first 91 games. Fast, daring, and with a devastating shot, at 18, Eto'o was the youngest player at the 1998 World Cup. Since then, he has become the first to be voted African soccer player of the year for three years in a row (2003–05). He was instrumental in Barcelona's 2006 Champions League success and in 2005/06, became the first striker in the top Spanish league for 15 years to score 50 goals over two seasons.

Defensive Duties

It may seem glamorous to be a striker but there is plenty of work apart from attacking for them to do. As part of the team, a striker has to be the first line of defense when his side loses the ball. He must chase and hassle the opposition defenders with the ball, closing them down and hoping to force them into a mistake or to intercept a pass. Strikers who are particularly good in the air often come back to help defend at corners and free kicks.

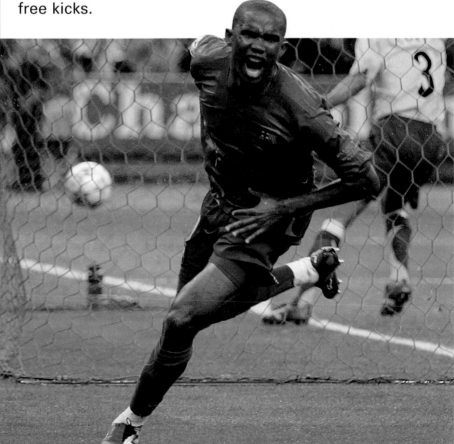

Samuel Eto'o celebrates scoring the equalizing goal during the 2006 Champions League final against Arsenal.

TACTICS

The way a team lines up, the style of soccer it plays, and the different moves and techniques it uses in attack and defense, are known as its tactics. The manager, or coach, is the person in charge of the team's tactics.

The Manager's Role

Tactics are chosen according to the strengths and the weaknesses the manager believes exist in the opposition. For instance, opponents whose defenders are large but slow might be best attacked with a number of fast forwards. Good tactics seek to use the skills of a team's best players to maximum advantage. For example, a team might support an in-form striker who is good in the air by playing wingers to deliver crosses to him. Sometimes a dangerous opponent will be man-marked by one player throughout a match to prevent him getting the ball and scoring. The manager not only chooses a team's tactics but also chooses the players who will start the game. He decides on the timing of substitutes, if any, which can change the course of a match.

TOP //// //// FACT

Juan Jose Tramutola was just 27 years old when he was head coach of Argentina at the 1930 World Cup.

Phil Scolari (Luiz Felipe Scolari), manager of 2002 World Cup winners Brazil, also took Portugal to the Euro 2004 final and to the 2006 World Cup semifinal.

Formations

The way in which a team lines up at the start of the game is known as its formation. This is usually given as the number of defenders, midfielders, and attackers lined up in banks across the field. For example, the common formation 4-4-2 consists of four defenders, four midfielders, and two attackers. Many managers and coaches have tried a variety of formations, including 4-3-3 with a three-man midfield and one or two wingers linking with the strikers. Other teams may opt for a 5-3-2 formation, with a five-man defense with wingbacks (see below) or a 4-4-1-1 formation, with a striker operating behind another one. Italy played this latter formation on their way to winning the 2006 World Cup. Teams may often switch formations in a game, for example, changing from 4-4-2 to 3-4-3 by using their substitutes to bring on another attacker. Some teams protecting a lead in the last minutes of a game opt to bring on an extra defensive midfielder and may switch to a 4-5-1 formation.

Tottenham Hotspur's Aaron Lennon skips past the tackle of Manchester City's Kiki Musampa during an English Premier League game. Fast and fit, Lennon can play as a wide midfielder or he can be used as a wingback, mixing defensive and attacking duties.

Wingbacks and Sweepers

There are also variations on the four-man defense. Some teams play a sweeper. This is an extra defender who covers the defense should an attack break through. Some sweepers play more of an attacking role, bringing the ball out of defense to become an extra player in midfield. A wingback is a cross between a wide midfielder and a fullback. Usually played as part of a 5-3-2 or 3-5-2 formation, these players need stamina to cover their side of the field in both defense and attack.

PASSING AND MOVEMENT

Passing the ball is the most important skill in soccer and helps a team to keep possession of the ball and build an attack. Passing must be accurate and at a height, speed, and angle that the player receiving the pass can control easily.

Short and Long

A soccer player can use different parts of his foot to propel the ball in different ways. The shortest but most accurate type of pass is when the inside of the foot (a sidefoot pass) is used to push or stroke the ball, usually along the ground. For small flicks to the side, a player may use the outside of his foot, while for longer passes, he tends to use the instep of his foot—where his shoelaces are. Whatever the length of the pass, it has to be hit with the right amount of force, otherwise it might be intercepted by an opponent or might overrun the intended target or go out of play. If the receiver is moving, the pass has to be played ahead of him so that he can run onto the ball.

Other Parts of the Body

In some situations, a player can make a pass using another part of his body besides his foot. A cushioned header, for example, sees the ball headed gently so that it drops to a teammate a few yards away. A flick-on header is played off the top of the head and is intended to pass the ball onto a teammate behind. The chest can also be used to bring down a ball and leave it at that player's feet, or to deflect the ball or push it back to another player on the same team.

Rising star Gareth Bale looks at his target as he makes a sidefoot pass. He strokes through the middle of the ball to make it skim across the field.

Who is...

...Zinedine Zidane?

Zinedine Zidane was one of the most accomplished passers in world soccer. One of a small, elite group of players to win the World Cup (1998) as well as the European Championship (2000), Zidane was able to spot passes other players could not and could thread a pass through the tiniest of gaps.

He was also a terrific free kick taker, goalscorer, and could run with the ball through defenses. His last World Cup match before retiring, the final of the 2006 competition, was blighted by his sending off for head-butting Marco Materazzi, but Zidane was controversially voted the player of the tournament.

Zinedine Zidane moves forward with the ball under control and his head up, looking for attacking options.

Movement

Passing works only if there are teammates who are in good positions to pass to. To create space and time in which to receive a pass, a player has to move away from any opponent marking him and be in a good position to receive and control the ball.

One commonly used pass-and-move technique is the wall pass. Here one player passes to another, then sprints forward to receive a return pass. This pair of passes can cut out an opposition defender who is in the way.

Another classic skill is for a player to dummy, or pretend that he is going to run one way when, in fact, he cuts away and runs in a different direction.

⚽ INDIVIDUAL SKILLS

Passing and movement are crucial individual skills for soccer players but there are other skills, too, that players need, including heading, dribbling, and tackling. A player must also learn to protect the ball by shielding it with his body and keeping his body between the ball and the opponent.

Tackling

Tackles can be made from the front, the side, or even from the back. In every case, the tackler has to be extremely careful to get the ball, to avoid fouling his opponent and to time his challenge perfectly. A fraction too early or too late and he may foul his opponent or his opponent may run away with the ball. The tackler's ideal aim is to win possession and move away with the ball. When this is not possible, he will try to prod the ball away out of his opponent's reach.

Heading

There is more than one type of header. An attacker aiming for goal needs to position himself above the ball so that he can aim the header downward. A defensive clearance header tends to be aimed higher and with plenty of power to propel the ball as far away as possible. Many headers are made under pressure from an opponent, so players try to time their leap to meet the ball at the highest point possible.

Cristiano Ronaldo performs a drag back, where he pulls the ball back behind his standing leg to change direction.

❓ Who is...

...Cristiano Ronaldo?

With loads of dribbling tricks, including stepovers and swerves, as well as pace to burn, Portuguese winger Cristiano Ronaldo is one of the most exciting attacking talents in European soccer. After transferring from Porto to Manchester United as a teenager in 2003, Ronaldo has improved his game dramatically to become a lethal attacker and home-crowd favorite. He scored Manchester United's 1,000th Premier League goal in 2005 and reached a World Cup semifinal and a European Championships final with Portugal.

TOP /////
///// FACT

England's 20-year old John Farnworth, a former Preston Town non-league player, won the World Freestyle Skills Championship in 2004. Farnworth also holds the world record for keeping a ball in the air just using headers for a staggering five hours, six minutes, and 30 seconds!

Dribbling

Dribbling involves moving with the ball and controlling it with a series of small kicks or taps. A straight dribble without any pace or variation can be easy to defend against. A good dribbler, therefore, adds various moves to his dribbling run, such as changes of pace and swerves, to make the dribble effective. A dummy and swerve move, for example, is where the dribbler threatens to move to one side of the defender by dropping his shoulder. When the defender begins to move in that direction, the dribbler swerves around him on the other side. Dribbling is a high-risk strategy but when performed in the opponents' half, it can sometimes lead to a goalscoring chance.

Sweden's Anna Sjoestroem shows good strength and technique to shield the ball and hold off the challenge of Nigeria's Florence Iweta.

⚽ATTACKING PLAY

A team attacks with the aim of getting the ball to a teammate in a position to score. With goals and attacking play vital to success, it is not surprising that most of the world's best-known players are attack-minded. Only one defender (Fabio Cannavaro) and one defensive midfielder (Lothar Matthäus) have ever won the FIFA World Player of the Year—the other winners have all been attacking midfielders or strikers.

Different Attacks

Attacks vary greatly. They can involve a player going it alone with a powerful, long-range shot or a dazzling weaving run. In an example of this, Maradona dribbled through the England defense to score his memorable 1986 World Cup goal. Attacks can also take time and involve many players. An example of this was the intricate 24-pass team move by Argentina at the 2006 World Cup, which led to Esteban Cambiasso scoring against Serbia and Montenegro. When one team's attack breaks down, many of its players may be out of position. This gives the other team the chance to launch a quick counterattack, either through fast running forward or via a long pass up the field to a striker. When the opposing team is back in defense, the attacking side may have to be patient and move the ball around, looking for players in space and an opening.

Shaktar Donetsk's Fernandinho goes on a swerving run during a 2006 Champions League match.

Space and Crosses

Attackers search for space on the field in which they can receive the ball and either build the attack further or take a shot on goal. Attackers can sometimes make space for each other by making a run that draws defenders toward them and creates a gap for a teammate. Skillful players try to make passes called through balls that travel behind the defenders and are placed for teammates to run onto.

Attackers, though, have to time their runs carefully so that they are not offside. Space sometimes appears near the sidelines and an overlapping run down the line can see a player get the ball. From this position, he can make a long pass, known as a cross, into the penalty area. Crosses, met by attackers using their heads or kicks of the ball in mid-air known as volleys, are a regular source of goals.

Wayne Rooney is an example of an attacker who often plays quite deep to get the ball from his midfield to surge at opponents, and unleash a long shot or a delicate through ball to release a teammate.

TOP FACT

Attacking players command high transfer fees. The biggest profit ever made by a club on one player was by Bordeaux. They bought Zinedine Zidane for $5.4 million and later sold him for $77.5 million.

Attacking Throw-ins

Teams often underestimate the importance of throw-ins. However, a quickly taken throw down the line, for example, can release a winger and allow him to make a cross. Some players have honed their long throws so well that a throw-in awarded deep in their opponent's half is almost the same as a corner with the player reaching the penalty area with his throw.

SET PIECES

Set pieces are devices by which the game is restarted after a foul, an infringement of the laws of the game, or after the ball has gone out of play. Defenders need to be alert to the dangers; over 20 percent of goals scored at the 1998 and 2002 World Cups, for example, were scored from set pieces such as corners and free kicks.

Shunsuke Nakamura takes one of his trademark swerving free kicks. The Japanese midfielder is one of the best free kick takers around and scored a memorable 2006 goal for his club, Celtic, versus Manchester United in the Champions League.

Corner Kicks

Corner kicks offer a free cross deep into the penalty area. The player taking the corner kick may look for another player to flick the corner onto at the near post or may play a corner short to a player free on the edge of the penalty area. Central defenders' height and skill in the air often sees them come up the field at corners and free kicks. Corner-takers can bend the ball in toward goal or outward, and a good corner kick is hit with pace, so that the slightest touch can deflect the ball toward the goal. Defenders try to mark up all their opponents in what can be a crowded area. They have to stay alert for last-second runs by attackers into their area.

Free Kicks

Some free kicks close to a team's own goal, or in the middle of the field, may be taken quickly with the ball pushed forward or to the side to start an attack. Free kicks closer to the opponents' goal offer greater attacking opportunities. The defending team usually arranges a "wall" that cannot be closer than 11 yd. (10 m) from the free kick. The attacking side has a number of options. A renowned swerver of the ball such as David Beckham, Ronaldinho, or Juninho Pernambucano can bend the ball up and over or around the wall and toward goal. Alternatively, the team may play the ball to the side so that another player with a strong shot has a clear view of the goal.

Arsenal's Dutch striker, Robin van Persie, takes a penalty against Charlton. Thierry Henry and the Charlton defenders look to follow up in case the ball is saved or rebounds off the post. They must not enter the penalty area until the taker has kicked the ball.

Penalties

Penalties are awarded for serious fouls or infringements inside a penalty area. The ball is placed just under 13 yd. (12 m) from the goal; a penalty kicked hard takes under half a second to reach the goal. A penalty is an excellent chance to score, but often the pressure becomes too much for some players who blast the ball high or wide or give the goalie the chance of a save. Goalies may move along their goal line before the kick is taken and can gamble on diving to one side or staying in the center of the goal for a penalty aimed down the middle.

Penalty Shootouts

A penalty shootout consists of a minimum of five penalties per team. It is the way many games are decided if they remain a draw after extra time has been played. Each team takes alternate penalties and, if the scores are level after the 10 penalties, pairs of players, one from each team, take penalties until one misses and one scores.

GOAL!

Goals win games. A team's tactics and attacking play must maximize the chances the team has to score. While free kicks and corner kicks are important, the majority of goals are scored with the ball on the move in open play.

Who is...

...Pele?

Pele is the nickname of the Brazilian, Edson Arantes Di Nascimento, who was one of, if not the, greatest-ever players in world soccer. A striker who played almost his entire career for the Brazilian club, Santos, Pele scored over 1,250 goals for club and country and was part of three World Cup winning squads (1958, 1962, and 1970). Possessing astonishing vision and skills, as well as strength and pace, Pele was a true goal-scoring machine, scoring a hat trick 93 times and notching four goals in a game a staggering 37 times.

Top goalscorers like Pele react to situations quickly, try to get to the ball first, and aim a shot out of reach of the goalkeeper.

Scoring Goals

Compared with other team sports, soccer is a low-scoring game. A single goal will often win a match. Teams may attack well, but without reliable players to bring home the chances they create, they will struggle. Whether bursting through from midfield or playing upfront, good goalscorers have a natural eye for the goal and must be sharp and aware of the game around them. Occasionally, they will see a teammate who is in a better position to score than they are and may attempt to pass the ball to him. However, most goalscorers take the chance themselves, reacting in an instant and choosing where to aim for and what sort of shot to use.

Some players are highly skilled at bending the ball and placing it in the upper or lower corners of the goal. Others opt for power and hit a drive with the instep of their shoe, trying to keep the ball down and on target. In many situations inside the penalty area, the ball falls to a goalscorer who must react that instant. A high-bouncing ball may be hit goalward by a diving header, a side volley, or, if the player's back is to goal, an overhead kick.

Stopping Shots

The defending team does its best to stop its opponents from getting a chance on goal. The team does this by dispossessing the player before he strikes, either by regaining possession, or, if under pressure, by clearing the ball away from danger. If their opponents get the chance to shoot, outfield players do their best to block the shot or header with any part of their bodies except their hands and arms. Now and then, a shot or cross hits a defender and deflects past the goalie to score an own goal.

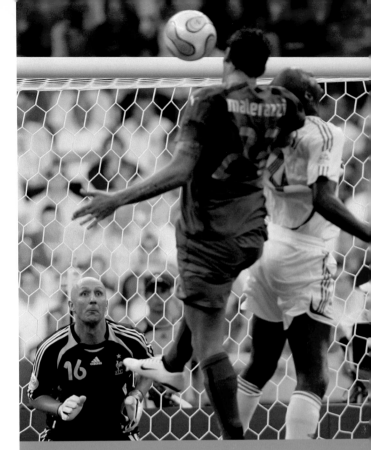

Italian defender Marco Materazzi leaps high during the 2006 World Cup final to score with a header. Central defenders are often good in the air and come up to attack their team's corners and free kicks.

STAT ATTACK

Top Five Male International Goalscorers

1. Ali Daei (Iran) 109 goals, 149 caps

2. Ferenc Puskás (Hungary and Spain) 84 goals, 89 caps

3. Pele (Brazil) 77 goals, 92 caps

4. Sándor Kocsis (Hungary) 75 goals, 68 caps

5. Bashar Abdullah (Kuwait) 75 goals, 134 caps

Stirring Comebacks

Goals can turn games around, so teams that are several goals behind strive not to give up but to double their efforts to score themselves. Pulling a goal back is crucial, since it can make the opposition defense jittery. It often leads to chances to score again. In the 2004/2005 Champions League final, for instance, Liverpool were 3–0 down at halftime. They staged a stunning comeback to draw 3–3 with AC Milan and then succeeded in the penalty shootout that followed to win the competition.

THE BIG COMPETITIONS

All professional soccer players, whether they are up-and-coming young players or experienced veteran professionals, want to play in the biggest matches possible. Some of these are massive club games such as top-of-the league-clashes or the final of a cup competition. Other matches involve soccer players playing for their country in international competitions.

International Appearances

Representing their country is a major achievement for players. Many matches played by international teams are friendlies designed to test out a team and let the manager try out different combinations of players in his side. Serious matches involve qualifying for the World Cup and major continental competitions such as the European Championships, the Copa America, or the African Cup of Nations. Many players, excellent at club level, fail to match their success at international level and manage only a handful of appearances, known as caps, for their country. Some star soccer players manage to perform at the highest level for many years and notch up a lot of caps. Such star players include England's David Beckham (115 caps), Italy's Paolo Maldini (126 caps), Portugal's Luis Figo (127 caps), and Brazil's veteran defender, Cafu (145 caps).

Didier Drogba playing for the Ivory Coast tries to bring the ball down during a 2006 African Cup of Nations against Gabon. The Ivory Coast won 5–0 on the way to becoming tournament runners-up behind Egypt.

Continental Competitions

Each continent has some form of major competition that features the best national teams in the region. In Asia, there are two competitions, the Asian Cup and soccer at the Asian Games, an event that features other sports, too. South America's Copa America began in 1910 and is the oldest of the continental competitions. It has traditionally seen the powerful soccer nations of Argentina (14 wins), Uruguay (14 wins), and Brazil (7 wins) triumph, although in 2001 Colombia provided a shock by winning. Only three teams took part in the first African Cup of Nations. The 2006 competition was hotly contested by more than 40 national teams; the final was won by Egypt.

Soccer at the Olympics

Soccer has appeared at the Summer Olympics officially since 1908, although tournaments connected to the Olympics were held in 1900 and 1904. For many years, it was a competition for amateur players but in the 1990s, the rules were relaxed to include mainly young, professional players. At the 2004 Olympics, for example, the Portugal team included a young Cristiano Ronaldo. The 1996 Games in Atlanta marked the first gold medal for African soccer with Nigeria's Super Eagles; it also saw the arrival of women's soccer at the Olympics. The home team, led by stars such as Kristine Lilly and Mia Hamm, won gold there and at the 2004 Athens Games.

STAT ATTACK

Recent Olympic Winners

Year	Men's	Women's
2008	Argentina	USA
2004	Argentina	USA
2000	Cameroon	Norway
1996	Nigeria	USA
1992	Spain	
1988	USSR	

Australia's Tim Cahill makes a tackle on Bahrain's Faouzi Aaish during a qualifying game for the 2007 Asian Cup. In 2006, Australia left Oceania to join the Asian Football Confederation. This means that Australia now takes part in the Asian Cup and will also try to qualify for the World Cup from groups in Asia.

CLUB SOCCER

Clubs are the core of soccer. Players play for amateur clubs and lower-level teams, dreaming of a move to a big club playing in one of the major leagues. Most major leagues feature a pyramid system, with teams able to rise and fall between divisions of a league through promotion and relegation.

The Big Leagues

Five leagues in Europe—Serie A in Italy, the Premier League in England, the Bundesliga in Germany, Spain's La Liga, and France's Le Championnat—are considered the most important leagues in the world. Their clubs are extremely wealthy and able to attract top players from all over the world. For example, players from more than 75 countries from Algeria to Zimbabwe have played in the English Premier League. The top 50 most expensive player transfers have all been of players bought by clubs in those five leagues. Within each of these big leagues, there is a handful of bigger clubs whose buying power has enabled them to win many league championships. For instance, in Spain, Real Madrid, and Barcelona have won 36 league titles between them while in Italy, Juventus, with 27 league titles, are Serie A's most successful team.

STAT ATTACK

Top Eight Average Attendances In Europe (2005–06)

1.	Barcelona	73,225
2.	Borussia Dortmund	72,625
3.	Real Madrid	71,545
4.	Manchester United	68,675
5.	Bayern Munich	67,640
6.	Schalke 04	61,300
7.	AC Milan	59,995
8.	Celtic	58,150

Bayern Munich midfielder Lukas Podolski runs with the ball during the opening game of the 2006/07 Bundesliga season against Borussia Dortmund. Bayern Munich had been crowned Bundesliga champions seven times in the previous ten seasons.

Who is...

...Thierry Henry?

Thierry Henry is a French World Cup and European Championship winner who, after his $18.7 million move from Italian team Juventus in 1999, played for Arsenal. After taking ten matches to score his first goal, this lethal striker had been the top scorer for his club until 2006. He became Arsenal's all-time leading goalscorer before transferring to FC Barcelona in mid-2007.

Thierry Henry lines up a shot for Arsenal as he is shadowed by Liverpool's Steven Gerrard during their 2007 FA Cup match. Arsenal has won the FA Cup a total of ten times.

Old and New

While some leagues have been running for a century or more, other countries have only recently introduced professional leagues. Japan's J-League began in 1993 and now has two divisions. Kashima Antlers, with 4 league titles, is its most successful team. Australia's A-League began in 2005 and features eight teams in a single league. In the United States, there has been a number of attempts to set up full-time professional leagues. WUSA, the women's professional league, was unfortunately stopped in 2003 but the male league, the MLS, has built a loyal following. In 2007, MLS team LA Galaxy announced a stunning swoop for David Beckham in a contract deal worth over $200 million.

Cup Competitions

In addition to league soccer, almost all soccer-playing nations have at least one cup competition that teams enter. The oldest and most famous club cup competition is the FA Cup in England. Held since the 1871/72 season, the FA Cup sees hundreds of amateur teams enter the preliminary rounds in August, hoping to get through rounds for a third round tie against a Premier League team. Ten teams have won the FA Cup five times or more; up until 2007, Manchester United is the leading team with 11 wins.

EUROPEAN COMPETITIONS

Whatever their nationality, many of the world's greatest players play for clubs in Europe. The continent is home of the world's richest clubs, such as Chelsea, Real Madrid, AC Milan, Bayern Munich, and Manchester United. European club competitions pit most of the world's best players against one another. For the national teams of Europe, the European Championship is second only to the World Cup in importance.

European Cups

There have been a number of cup competitions for European clubs including the Inter-Toto Cup, the European Cup Winners' Cup, and the UEFA Cup. The European Cup, which began in 1956, was the most prestigious. Dominated at first by Real Madrid, who won an incredible five European Cups in a row, the competition saw the winners of national leagues play knockout pairs of matches, one at home, one away. The winner of each pair of games progressed to the next round. During the 1960s and 1970s, there were periods where teams won two or three European Cups in a row, but the 1980s was very competitive and saw teams from Eastern Europe win for the first time.

Spanish striker Raul played for Real Madrid in the Champions League. With 323 goals as of July 2010, Raul is the highest-ever scorer in the Champions League.

Champions League

In the 1992/93 season, the European Cup was repackaged into a new format, with small groups of teams playing one another in mini-leagues before entering home and away knockout games leading to the final. Despite criticisms of too many meaningless games, television rights have made the Champions League an incredibly wealthy competition to be a part of. A club that qualifies for the following season's competition by finishing high enough in its league can earn tens of millions of dollars. Teams from England, Italy, Spain, France, Portugal, Germany, and the Netherlands have all won the Champions League, which has seen some epic games in recent years. These include Dynamo Kiev's 4–2 victory over Bayer Leverkusen and Barcelona's 2–1 win over Arsenal in the 2006 final.

European Championships

The idea of a tournament between the national teams of Europe had been around for half a century before the European Championships began in 1960. After experimenting with different formats, the tournament is now held once every four years, with 16 teams from the 50 or so that attempt to qualify. Euro 2004 was held in Portugal with the hosts reaching the final. They were beaten by Greece, the surprise team of the tournament.

Germany's Renate Lingor heads the ball away from Norway's Solveig Gulbrandsen during the Final of the Women's Euro 2005 tournament.

STAT ATTACK

Women's European Championships Winners

2003–2005	Germany
1999–2001	Germany
1995–1997	Germany
1993–1995	Germany
1991–1993	Norway
1989–1991	Germany
1987–1989	Germany
1984–1987	Norway
1982–1984	Sweden

THE WORLD CUP

The FIFA World Cup is the ultimate prize in soccer. From small beginnings, where 13 teams contested the 1930 competition, the tournament has grown to become the biggest single sports event in the world. The 2010 World Cup's 64 games were watched live by millions of spectators and an estimated cumulative television audience of over 6 billion.

Qualification

The World Cup is held every four years and now has 32 of the world's best teams in the tournament, known as the finals. The qualification process begins several years in advance when around 200 soccer-playing nations attempt to qualify to play in the finals. Qualifying can be tough and the fans of many major soccer nations are disappointed when their team does not make it through. Dutch fans, for instance, were distraught when their team failed to qualify for the 2002 tournament, while Portugal has appeared at only four of the 18 World Cups.

The Brazilian captain, Cafu, kisses the World Cup trophy after his team beat Germany 2–0 in the 2002 final. Brazil beat England, Belgium, and Turkey in both the group and knockout stages, on the way to the final.

STAT ATTACK

World Cup Winners

5 Brazil (1958, 1962, 1970, 1994, 2002)

4 Italy (1934, 1938, 1982, 2006)

3 Germany (1954, 1974, 1990)

2 Argentina (1978, 1986)

2 Uruguay (1930, 1950)

1 Spain (2010)

1 France (1998)

1 England (1966)

Successful Teams

Teams from South America and Europe have won all the World Cup competitions. However, in recent years, nations from elsewhere in the world have improved. South Korea reached the semifinal of the 2002 World Cup and there have been strong showings from Japan, Ghana, Australia, and the United States. Only Brazil has appeared at all 18 tournaments and is the most successful World Cup nation with seven appearances in the final. Brazil has won five World Cups, and has the longest unbeaten run of 13 games between 1958 and 1966 and the longest run of wins—11 at the 2002 and 2006 tournaments.

TOP //// //// FACT

During the 1938 World Cup, Italy's Giuseppe Meazza was about to take a penalty when his shorts fell down. Coolly grasping the shorts with one hand, he scored the penalty that took Italy into the final, which they won.

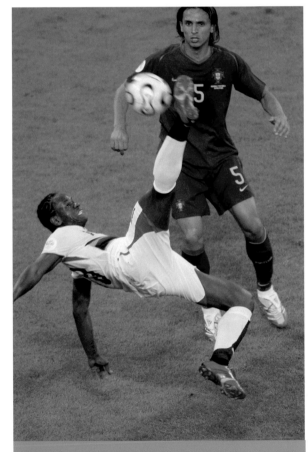

Angola's Fabrice Akwa makes a spectacular overhead kick during the 2006 World Cup match against eventual semifinalists, Portugal.

Scoring Feats

There have been many goals scored at the World Cup. In fact, it was not until 1958 at the Brazil versus England match that the World Cup tournament experienced a 0-0 draw. At the 2006 World Cup, Sweden's Marcus Allbäck scored the 2,000th World Cup goal. The player who scores the most goals at a World Cup is awarded the Golden Boot. Germany's Miroslav Klose, who scored five goals, won the 2006 Golden Boot. Brazil's Ronaldo won the 2002 Golden Boot and holds the record of most goals scored in World Cup finals—15 in total.

Although in modern times, matches have become tighter, the occasional high-scoring game does occur. Costa Rica lost to Brazil in a 5–2 thriller in 2002 and followed it up at the 2006 World Cup with a 4–2 loss to the hosts, Germany, who had thrashed Saudi Arabia 8–0 in 2002. As the 2006 tournament progressed, games became much closer. Four games went to penalty shootouts that knocked out France, England, Argentina, and Switzerland in the process.

WORLD CUP LEGENDS

The sport of soccer has generated dozens of brilliant individual players, some of whom have been able to shine at the FIFA World Cup. Here are five players who have had a major impact on the tournament.

Diego Maradona

Short, stocky but incredibly gifted, Maradona played at four World Cups. It was the 1986 tournament in which he really shined, as his amazing dribbling skills and eye for goal propelled an otherwise unremarkable Argentina team to win the World Cup. He then captained Argentina to the final of the 1990 competition, losing to Germany, before failing two drugs tests (1991, 1994) that saw the end of his international career.

Ronaldo

A veteran of four World Cups and winner of two (1994, 2002), Ronaldo is a striker who, for a decade, was one of the most frequent scoring players in Europe. He scored 47 goals in 49 games for Barcelona, 49 in 68 games for Inter Milan, and almost 70 goals in his time at Real Madrid. Returning after serious injury, he was the top-scorer at the 2002 World Cup and holds the record for the most World Cup finals goals. With 62 goals for his country, he is Brazil's second-highest goalscorer of all time.

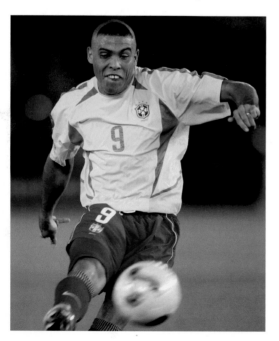

TOP //// //// FACT

With a reputed age of 42, Cameroon striker Roger Milla, became the oldest player to both appear and score in a World Cup when he struck at the 1994 tournament.

Just Fontaine

Frenchman Just Fontaine played in only one World Cup, the 1958 tournament, but had a huge impact. He started the tournament out of the side, but injury to another attacker gave him his chance. He took it, scoring an amazing 13 goals in just six games. He still remains the highest goalscorer in a single World Cup. Injury in 1962 ended his career, by which time he had scored 165 goals in the French League in just 200 matches.

Franz Beckenbauer

German soccer player Franz Beckenbauer played in three World Cups, reaching the final twice, and winning the 1974 tournament and the semifinal once. A stylish defender or midfielder, Beckenbauer was comfortable on the ball and turned the position of sweeper into a more attacking one, linking with midfield. He played almost 400 games for one club, Bayern Munich, and got 103 caps with the German national team. He later became manager of Germany and led them to victory in the 1990 World Cup.

STAT ATTACK

FIFA World Player of the Year

Year	Player
1993	Roberto Baggio (Italy)
1994	Romário (Brazil)
1995	George Weah (Liberia)
1996	Ronaldo (Brazil)
1997	Ronaldo (Brazil)
1998	Zinedine Zidane (France)
1999	Rivaldo (Brazil)
2000	Zinedine Zidane (France)
2001	Luis Figo (Portugal)
2002	Ronaldo (Brazil)
2003	Zinedine Zidane (France)
2004	Ronaldinho (Brazil)
2005	Ronaldinho (Brazil)
2006	Fabio Cannavaro (Italy)
2007	Kaka (Brazil)
2008	Cristiano Ronaldo (Portugal)
2009	Lionel Messi (Argentina)

Johann Cruyff

The key player in the great Netherlands teams of the 1970s, Johann Cruyff was an incredibly skillful and intelligent soccer player. Technically a striker, Cruyff would pop up all over the field linking play, creating chances for teammates, and scoring crucial goals. His return of 33 goals in just 48 caps for the Netherlands would have been higher had it not been for his refusal to play at the 1978 World Cup. At club level, Cruyff was a major part of Dutch team Ajax's success as they won three European Cups in a row.

GLOSSARY

Back-pass rule The rule in soccer that means that a deliberate pass backward by a player to his goalkeeper cannot be handled by the goalie.

Caps The appearances for his national team in international matches that a top player may make.

Clearance Kicking or heading the ball out of defense.

Counterattack When one team's attack breaks down and the other team starts to attack right afterward.

Cross Sending the ball from the sideline to the center of the field, usually into the other team's penalty area.

Cushioning Slowing a ball down to control it by using a part of the body.

Dummy Pretending to move one way to trick an opponent but actually moving in another direction.

Extra time The time added on at the end of a soccer game when the score is tied at the end of full time.

FIFA Stands for the Fédération Internationale de Football Association, the international governing body of soccer.

Formation The way in which a team lines up on the field. The formation is usually given in numbers of defenders, midfielders, and strikers, for example 4-4-2.

Friendlies International or club games played outside of a full competition.

Hand ball The illegal use of the hand or arm by a player.

Hat trick To score three goals in a game.

Instep The part of the shoe where the laces are.

Intercept When one team tries to pass the ball and an opponent moves and obtains it.

Jockeying The skill of delaying an opponent with the ball.

Man-marking Where a defender guards an opponent to try to stop him getting the ball.

Merchandise Ranges of product, from buttons to mugs and shirts sold by clubs to fans.

Outfield A term that refers to all players on the field, other than the two goalkeepers.

Overlap To run outside and beyond a teammate down the sides of the field in order to create space and a possible passing opportunity.

Pens The abbreviation used in scoring to show that the game was won on penalties.

Stamina The ability to maintain physical effort over long periods. All players require good levels of stamina to stay effective over an entire match.

Substitution When a player is replaced on the field by another, fresh player.

USSF Stands for the United States Soccer Federation, the body that runs soccer in the U.S.

Volleying When the ball is kicked while in mid-air and before it bounces.

Zonal marking When a defender marks an area of the field instead of marking a single opponent.

FURTHER READING

Soccer: The Ultimate Guide
by Martin Cloake
(DK Publishing, 2010)

The Complete Encyclopedia of Soccer
by Keir Radnedge
(Carlton Books, 2009)

The Everything Kids' Soccer Book
by Deborah W. Crisfield
(Adams Media, 2009)

A Beautiful Game: The World's Greatest Players and How Soccer Changed Their Lives
by Tom Watt
(HarperOne, 2010)

Science Behind Sports: Soccer
by Jennifer MacKay
(Lucent Books, 2011)

The World's Greatest Soccer Players
by Matt Doeden
(Capstone Press, 2010)

WEB SITES

Due to the changing nature of Internet links, Rosen Publishing has developed an online list of Web sites related to the subject of this book. This site is regularly updated. Please use this link to access this list: http://www.rosenlinks.com/sw/soc

INDEX